THE CAFETERIA

THE CAFETERIA

Based on the story by Isaac Bashevis Singer,
Adapted by Rhys Adrian

ISAAC BASHEVIS SINGER

Cast of Characters
(in order of appearance)

Aaron . . . . a Yiddish writer
Lieberman . . . . . . an old man
Paul . . . . . a middle-aged man
Esther . . . . a young Holocaust survivor
Father . . . . an elderly man, amputated below the knee
Rabbi . . . . . a middle-aged man with a short beard

Sets
(in order of appearance)

A cafeteria
Esther's place
Aaron's apartment
Phone booth
Subway
Train

The following adaptation of Isaac Bashevis Singer's story, "The Cafeteria," appeared on BBC2 Playhouse on August 13, 1974. It is being reproduced in this Playsmith edition as a one-act to be performed on a bare stage with furniture and props. The scenes are indicated by numbers. Minor edits have been made for the sake of live performance.

1. A cafeteria.

Narration: "Even though I reached the point where a great part of my earnings is given away in taxes, I still have the habit of eating in cafeterias when I am by myself. I like to take a tray and choose from the counter the food I enjoy. Besides, I meet there the landsleit from Poland, as well as all kinds of literary beginners and readers who know Yiddish. The moment I sit down at a table, they come over, saying, 'Hello, Aaron,' and we talk about Yiddish litera-ture, the Holocaust, and the State of Israel.'"

Aaron is sitting at a table reading a newspaper. Lieberman, who sees Aaron, is quite frail. He sees Aaron and crosses to his table with a glass of tea.

Lieberman	Aaron.
Aaron	David.
Lieberman	May I join you?
Aaron	Of course, please.
Lieberman	It's good to see you again.

Aaron	It's good to see you, too.
Lieberman	Someone said you went to Tel Aviv.
Aaron	I went to California. To Los Angeles. Toronto.
Lieberman	You still lecture?
Aaron	These days I seem to spend more and more of my life traveling.
Lieberman	Anyway. It is good to see you. How long have you been back?
Aaron	Two weeks. I looked out for you. But you haven't come.
Lieberman	I don't get out as much. Too much noise. And the sidewalk—it's too much of a rush.
Aaron	Not so many of the old faces here. Few I recognize.
Lieberman	There have been changes, of course. Someone disappears and I think he's already in the next world. Suddenly he reappears and tells me he has tried to settle in Tel Aviv or Los Angeles. He has a few more wrinkles, but he tells the same stories with the same gestures, as though life has not moved. How long is it since you've been away?
Aaron	This time? Nine months.
Lieberman	I envy your life, Aaron. If I were a writer, successful like you, I would live in Tel Aviv.
Aaron	I put my roots down here. I'm too old now to put them down elsewhere.

	I've lived here as long as I've lived in Poland. Thirty years. I know every inch from 96th Street to 72nd Street. From Central Park to Riverside Drive. There are so many memories.
Lieberman	You remember the old refugee from Poland. He used to sit there. A translator. He died three months ago. Stopped coming. Then someone said he was dead.
Aaron	What was his name?
Lieberman	I never knew his name. He used to sit there quietly. Working.
Aaron	I seem to remember someone sitting there. Writing. But maybe I'm thinking of someone else.
Lieberman	I begin to ask myself. Who's next? One day this place will have to close. The young keep away. Old men and their quarrels. Intrigues and pettiness it's better not to know about. But with you, we keep in touch, we read your articles. Do you have another novel coming?
Aaron	I'm finishing one. With luck it should come out next year.
Lieberman	None of us learns from these deaths. Old age doesn't cleanse us. We don't repent.

Lights down.

2. Cafeteria. It is some time in the early 1950s. The owners are elderly, their hair gray, and there are perhaps one or two GIs among the customers. Lights up on Esther at a table, surrounded by admirers, all older men. She is very animated and talks and laughs and entertains the men.

Narration: "It was in the early fifties that a woman appeared in the cafeteria, younger than the rest of us. She had been in a prison camp in Russia and had spent some time in the DP camps in Germany before getting a visa for the United States. The men all hovered around her. They didn't let her pay. They listened to her talk and tell jokes. They gallantly bought her coffee and cheesecake. She had returned from the devastation and was still joyful. One day she looked across at me and smiled, and from that moment I imagined I was in love with her."

We see Esther whisper to one of her companions who looks across at Aaron. He nods and they both stand up and cross to Aaron's table.

Paul	Aaron, you're a lucky man. This young lady is an admirer. She wished to be introduced to you. Esther. Aaron.
Aaron	How do you do?
Esther	May I sit?
Aaron	Of course. Please.
Paul	I'll leave you together. But, Aaron, don't take her from us.

Paul goes back to his group.

Esther	You're my writer.
Aaron	For such words I must kiss you.
Esther	What are you waiting for?

She leans forward and kisses his cheek.

Aaron	Esther. You're a fireball.
Esther	Yes, fire from Gehenna. I have been trying to get the courage to speak to you for days. Since I found out who you were. I read your books in Poland. And while in the DP camps in Germany after the war. They kept me going.
Aaron	You flatter me.
Esther	And now I am sitting here with you. It's almost a miracle.
Aaron	Young people don't come here much. Why do you come?
Esther	I like to hear the old men talk about Poland. And now I'm with you and I can think of nothing to say.
Aaron	Say nothing. *He looks at her.* What do you do?
Esther	I work in a factory. In New Jersey. I sort buttons.
Aaron	You should find a better job.
Esther	It suits me. I would like to ask you for a favor.

Aaron	Of course.
Esther	My father is also an admirer of yours. He's also read your books. He would very much like to meet you. But he's confined. He can't go out. Would you visit us?
Aaron	Yes.
Esther	When?
Aaron	One day.
Esther	Why not now?
Aaron	Now?
Esther	You're sitting here drinking coffee. You could be sitting there drinking coffee. Will you come?
Aaron	All right. There's nothing else I have to do.

They get up from their seats

| Aaron | Esther. You're a remarkable young woman. |

3. Esther's place.

It is somber and poor. The living room is probably where Esther sleeps while her father likely sleeps in the other room, which we won't see. A small cramped kitchen with ancient equipment. Esther is in the kitchen. She has flowers in her hand. She smells them.

Aaron is in the living room next to Esther's father, who sits in a wheelchair. His legs have been amputated below the knee. He looks like a strong man, with a head of thick white hair, a ruddy face, and eyes full of energy.

Father	In the living room. Daughter! Where's the tea?

Looks around the kitchen door.

Esther	Wait. I'm arranging the flowers.
Father	You bring home a guest and already you desert him.
Esther	Father. The kettle has to boil.

She disappears back into the kitchen.

Aaron	I am glad to have come. And glad to have met you.
Father	I've read your books. Did Esther tell you?
Aaron	She did. I'm flattered.
Father	Except when I was in Russia. There were no books there. But I survived. Not many did. *He laughs.* I escaped from Warsaw for freedom in Russia. Back to the old country. It was 1939. There was no time. We had to get out quick. Just Esther and myself. My wife and the other children stayed in Warsaw. I thought I could carry on the fight from Russia. Do you see? A good Communist. A functionary

in the party. And look what happened. In Russia I was denounced as a Trotskyite! *He gives a laugh.* Me! Some informer, some party functionary, didn't like how I looked. Or how I walked. Or how I smiled. Or how I scratched the side of my head. They sent me to mine coal in the north. The GPU sent people there to die. Even the strongest couldn't survive the cold and hunger for more than a year. But my legs froze. The surgeon was a butcher. *A very slight pause.* Exiled without a sentence. Zionists, Bundists, members of the Polish Socialist Party, just refugees, all because of the labor shortage. They died together. Scurvy. Beriberi. But isn't it a joke? Stalinists? Bandits! Bootlickers! Outcasts! If not for the United Stated, Hitler would have run over all of Russia. *He smiles at Aaron as if to apologize.* We don't get many visitors.

Aaron   It's quite all right.

Father   We'd pick lice off each other. Or some of us would. Lice do not die in the cold. They die when the host dies.

Esther has entered the room with the vase of flowers. She puts them on the table.

Esther	Father! Enough.
Father	What's the matter? Am I lying?
Esther	One can have enough even of kreplach.
Father	Daughter. You had to do it, too.
Esther	Give Aaron a chance to speak. You are talking him over.
Aaron	It's all right.
Esther	Now I can make the tea.

She goes back to the kitchen. The father waits for her to go.

Father	She had a husband in Russia.
Aaron	I didn't know.
Father	A Polish Jew. He volunteered for the Red Army. Died.
Aaron	She should find herself someone here.
Father	She has. Or rather the other way. Someone here found her a refugee. A former smuggler in Germany. But now he is here. He has a book binding factory and has become rich. But she says she is not interested. *He leans forward.* Persuade her to marry him. It would be good for me, too.
Aaron	Maybe she doesn't love him.
Father	There is no such thing as love. Give me a cigarette.

Aaron gives him a cigarette, lights it for him. The father draws deeply on the cigarette, exhales.

Father   In the camp. People climbed one another like worms.

Lights down.

Narration:"I left, inviting Esther to supper a few days later, but she called to say that she had the flu and had to stay in bed. Then a situation arose that made me leave for Israel. I wanted to write to her but had lost her address. When I returned to New York I tried to call her, but there was no telephone listing for her or her father. Weeks passed and she didn't show up in the cafeteria. One evening I went to the cafeteria with the premonition that Esther would be there. I saw a black wall and barred windows. The cafeteria had burned down. The old men would now have to meet in another cafeteria. But where? To search is not in my nature. I had plenty of complications without Esther…. The summer passed. And late one day, I walked by the cafeteria and again saw lights, a counter, guests. The owners had rebuilt. And I saw Esther sitting alone at a table. She didn't notice me and I watched her for a while. She looked pale, as though recuperating from an illness."

4. The rebuilt cafeteria. Lights up on Esther sitting alone at a table. She wears a fez and a jacket with a faded fur collar. Aaron enters the cafeteria and crosses to her table.

Aaron   Esther!

Esther	*She starts and smiles.* Miracles do happen.
Aaron	What's new in buttons?
Esther	Where have you been?
Aaron	Where have *you* been?
Esther	I thought you were still abroad.
Aaron	I've been back since the spring. But you deserted us. I asked after you but no one has seen you all summer. I thought perhaps you'd gotten married.
Esther	No.
Aaron	Where are our cafeterianiks?
Esther	They now go to the cafeteria on 57th Street and Eighth Avenue. They only reopened this place yesterday. I don't suppose word has gotten around yet.
Aaron	May I bring you a cup of coffee?
Esther	I drink too much coffee. *She smiles at him.* But all right.

He crosses to the counter and gets the coffee. While he stands at the counter he looks across at her. She takes off her hat and smooths her hair. She then tilts the other chair against the table as a sign that the seat is taken. He returns with the coffee.

Aaron	It's good to see you again, Esther.
Esther	*She smiles.* You went abroad without saying goodbye …
Aaron	I lost your address …

Esther	… and there I was about to knock on the pearly gates of heaven.
Aaron	What happened?
Esther	Oh, the flu turned into pneumonia. They gave me penicillin, and I'm one of those who cannot take it. I got a rash all over my body. My father, too, is not well.
Aaron	What's the matter with him?
Esther	He has high blood pressure. He had a kind of stroke and his mouth has become crooked. He can't even do now for himself what he used to be able to do.
Aaron	Esther, I'm sorry.

An awkward pause

Aaron	Do you still work with buttons?
Esther	Yes, with buttons. At least I don't have to use my head, only my hands. I can think my own thoughts.
Aaron	What do you think about?
Esther	Whatever comes into my mind. The other workers are all Puerto Ricans. They rattle away in Spanish from morning to night.
Aaron	Who takes care of your father?
Esther	Who? Nobody. I come home in the evening to make supper. He's sleeping now, so I came out. He has one

	desire—to marry me off for my own good, and, perhaps, for his comfort. But I can't marry a man I don't love.
Aaron	What is love?
Esther	You ask me! You write novels about it. But you're a man—I assume you don't know what it really is. A woman is a piece of merchandise to you. To me a man who talks nonsense or smiles like an idiot is repulsive.
Aaron	Your bookbinder?
Esther	You know about him? I would rather die than live with him. A man who goes from one woman to another is not for me. I don't want to share with anybody.
Aaron	I'm afraid a time is coming when everybody will.
Esther	That is not for me.
Aaron	What kind of person was your husband?
Esther	How did you know I had a husband? My father, I suppose. The minute I leave the room, he talks. My husband believed in things and was ready to die for them. He was not exactly my type, but I respected him and loved him too. He wanted to die and died like a hero. What else can I say?
Aaron	And the others?
Esther	What others? There were no others. Men were after me. The way people

behaved in the war—you will never know. They lost all shame. On the bunks near me one time, a mother lay with one man and her daughter with another. People were like beasts—worse than beasts. *She smiles.* In the middle of it all, I dreamed about love. Now I have even stopped dreaming. The men who come here are terribly bored. Most of them are half crazy, too.

Aaron   You didn't always think that.

Esther   I do now. Once, one of them tried to read me a forty page poem. I almost fainted.

Aaron   I wouldn't read you anything I'd written.

Esther   I've been told how you behave—no!

Aaron   No is no. Drink your coffee.

Esther   You don't even try to persuade me. Most men here bother you and you can't get rid of them. In Russia people suffered, but I never met as many maniacs there as in New York City. The building where I live is a madhouse. My neighbors are lunatics. They sing, they cry, they break things. One of them jumped out of the window and killed herself. She was having an affair with a boy twenty years younger. In Russia, the problem was to escape lice and somehow to keep warm. Here you're surrounded by insanity.

A pause.

Aaron	Men and women will never really understand one another.
Esther	I cannot understand my own father. Sometimes he's a complete stranger to me. He won't live long.
Aaron	Is he so sick?
Esther	It's everything together. He's lost the will to live. Why live without legs, without friends, without a family? They've all perished. He sits and reads newspapers all day long. He acts as though he were interested in what's going on in the world. His ideals are gone, but he still hopes for a just revolution. How can a revolution help him? I myself never put my hopes in any movement or party. How can we hope when everything ends in death?
Aaron	Hope in itself is proof that there is no death.
Esther	Yes, I know. You often write about this. For me, death is the only comfort. What do the dead do? They continue to drink coffee and eat egg cookies? They still read newspapers? A life after death would be nothing but a joke.

Lights down.

Narration: "Sometimes months passed between my visits to the cafeteria. A year or two had gone by (perhaps three or four. I lost count.) and Esther did not show up. I had given her my telephone number should she ever need it, but she never rang. I asked about her a few times. Someone said she was going to a cafeteria on Forty-second Street. another heard that she was married. Someone else said she had moved to Chicago. ... Not many of the cafeterianiks had come back to the re-built cafeteria. New people appeared – all of them European. They had long discussions in Yiddish, Polish, Russian, even Hebrew. They asked to have their coffee in glasses, and held lumps of sugar between their teeth when they drank. Many of them were my readers. They introduced themselves and reproached me for all kinds of literary errors: that I contradicted myself, went too far in descriptions of sex, described Jews in such a way that anti-semites could use it for propaganda. ... I was to see Esther again. but her face told of the time that had passed. Her gaze was no longer clear. Around her mouth was an expression that could be called bitterness, disenchantment."

5. The cafeteria. Lights up on Lieberman and Aaron at a table. Lieberman now looks a little older than he did at the beginning of the play.

Lieberman	All sorts of different people here now. I don't have a taste for the place so much.
Aaron	After the fire it was bound to change.

Someone walks past their table with a coffee and a bowl of rice pudding. He sits at a nearby table.

Lieberman	You see that fellow. In Russia, he immediately became a Stalinist. He denounced his own friends. Here in America, he has switched to anti-Bolshevism.
Aaron	How do you know?
Lieberman	So I've been told.
Aaron	By whom?
Lieberman	By someone whose word I believe in.

The man knows he is being talked about. Lieberman reaches for his hat.

Aaron	You have to go?
Lieberman	It's late. I find comfort now in getting to bed early. I like to read. In bed. Aaron, I'll see you again soon.

Lieberman goes. The man at the other table stares at Aaron. After a pause he picks up his coffee and bowl of rice and crosses to Aaron's table.

Avrom	Don't believe a word of what you're told.
Aaron	I'm told nothing.
Avrom	They invent all sorts of lies. What could you do in a country where the rope was always around your neck. You had

to adjust yourself if you wanted to live and not die somewhere in Kazakhstan. To get a bowl of soup or a place to stay, you had to sell your soul.

Avrom indicates a table across the room where a few men are sitting. A man with a beard whispers into the ear of his companion who laughs.

Avrom	That table there. The man with the beard. He had a store in Auschwitz.
Aaron	What do you mean?
Avrom	God help us. He kept his merchandise in the straw where he slept—a rotten potato, sometimes a piece of soap, a tin spoon, a little fat. Still, he did business. Later, in Germany, he became such a big smuggler they once took forty thousand dollars from him.

Aaron sees Esther enter the cafeteria. She goes straight to the counter without seeing him.

Aaron	*To Avrom.* Excuse me, but I see an old friend.

He picks up his hat and coat and crosses to the counter.

Aaron	Esther. *She smiles, but her smile immediately faded away.* What happened to you?

Esther	Oh, I'm still alive.
Aaron	Please. Sit down. *He leads her to a different table from the one he just left.* May I get you a coffee?
Esther	If you insist.

She lights a cigarette and draws deeply on it. She opens her paper and glances at it. He returns with her coffee.

Aaron	You've gone over to the enemy.
Esther	What do you mean?
Aaron	It was a joke.
Esther	What kind of joke?
Aaron	The newspaper. It's the competitor to the paper to which I sometimes contribute. You've deserted me.
Esther	I see.
Aaron	Where were you all this time? I've asked about you.
Esther	Really? Well, thank you.
Aaron	What happened?
Esther	Nothing good. *She looks him over.* You have no hair, but you're pale.

A pause.

Aaron	You father?
Esther	He's been dead for almost a year.
Aaron	I'm sorry…
Esther	Don't be.

A pause.

Aaron	Do you still sort buttons?
Esther	No. I became an operator in a dress shop.
Aaron	And what happened to you personally, if I may ask?
Esther	Oh, nothing. Absolutely nothing. *She looks at him with a faint smile.* You won't believe it, but I was sitting at home this afternoon thinking of you. And here you are. I think I've fallen into some kind of trap. I don't know what to call it. I thought perhaps you could advise me.
Aaron	If I can.
Esther	If you can. Yes.
Aaron	Tell me.
Esther	You still have the patience to listen to the troubles of little people like me? I'm sorry. I didn't mean to insult you. I even doubted you would remember me if you saw me again.
Aaron	Of course I would remember you.
Esther	To make it short, I work but work is growing more difficult for me. I feel as if my bones might crack. I wake up in the morning and I can't sit up. One doctor tells me it's a disc in my back, others try to cure my nerves. One

took x-rays and said I had a tumor. He wanted me to go into hospital for a few days, but I'm in no hurry for such an operation. Suddenly a little lawyer shows up. He's a refugee himself and is connected with the German government. You know they are now giving reparation money? *He nods his head.* It's true that I escaped to Russia, but I am a victim of the Nazis just the same. Besides, they don't know my biography exactly. I could get a pension plus a few thousand dollars, but my dislocated disc is no good for the purpose because I got it later—after the camps.

Aaron   I don't see what you can do...

Esther   This lawyer says my only chance is to convince them that I am ruined psychically. It's the bitter truth, but how can you prove it? The German doctors, the neurologists, the psychiatrists require proof. Everything has to be according to the text books— just so and no different. The lawyer wants me to play insane. Naturally he gets twenty percent of the reparation money—maybe more. He's already in his seventies, an old bachelor. He tried to make love to me. He's half

21

meshuga himself. *She looks at him.* How can I play insane when I actually am insane. *He looks downwards.* The whole thing revolts me and I'm afraid it really will drive me crazy. I hate swindles. But this shyster pursues me. I don't sleep. When the alarm rings in the morning, I wake up as shattered as I used to be in Russia when I had to walk to the forest and chop wood at four in the morning. Of course I take sleeping pills—if I didn't, I wouldn't sleep at all. That is more or less the situation.

Aaron Esther. You are still a good looking woman. Why don't you get married?

Esther Well, the old question—there is nobody. It's too late. If you knew how I felt, you wouldn't ask such a question.

He moves his hand as if to touch her but doesn't. Lights down.

Narration: "Weeks passed. Snow had been falling. The sky above the roofs shone violet, without a moon, without stars, and even though it was eight o'clock in the evening the light and the emptiness reminded me of dawn. For a moment I had the feeling I was in Warsaw. The telephone rang and I rushed to answer it as I did ten, twenty, thirty years ago—still expecting the good tidings that a telephone call was about to bring me."

6. Aaron's apartment as Esther speaks from a pay booth.

Aron	Hello.
Esther	Aaron?
Aaron	Yes.
Esther	Excuse me for disturbing you. It's Esther. From a few weeks ago at the cafeteria.
Aaron	Esther!
Esther	I don't know how I got the courage to phone you. I need to talk to you about something. Naturally, if you have the time. And—please forgive my presumption.
Aaron	No presumption. Of course, you're welcome. Would you like to come to my apartment?
Esther	If I will not be interrupting. It's difficult to talk in the cafeteria. It's noisy and there are eavesdroppers. What I want to tell you is so secret I wouldn't want to trust it to anyone else.
Aaron	Do you know my address?
Esther	Yes.
Aaron	Are you far away?
Esther	I am quite near.
Aaron	Please come up.
Esther	Thank you.

Lights down as Esther hangs up and Aaron after her.

Narration: "I tried to make order in my apartment, but it was impossible. Letters, manuscripts lay around on tables and chairs. In the corners books and magazines were piled high. I opened the closets and threw inside whatever was under my hand: jackers, pants, shirts, shoes. I heard a bell ring and didn't know if it was the door or the telephone. I opened the door and saw Esther. I asked her in, and my neighbor, the divorcee, who spied on me openly and without shame – and, God knows, with no sense of purpose – opened her door and stared at my guest."

7. Aaron's apartment. There is snow on her hat and her shoulders. She takes off her hat and coat and hands it to him.

Esther   Thank you.

He moves some manuscripts off a sofa for her to sit.

Aaron   I'm sorry. In my house it's sheer chaos, as you can see.

Esther   It doesn't matter.

Aaron   Can I get you anything? I have some cognac.

Esther   No.

He sits, awkward.

Aaron   Did you walk here?

Esther   Yes.

Aaron   It's dangerous to walk alone on the streets of New York at night.

Esther	What would it matter?
Aaron	It would matter. *Pause.* You're not cold.
Esther	No. *Pause.* Do you remember the time I spoke to you about my lawyer—that I had to go to a psychiatrist because of the reparation money?
Aaron	Yes.
Esther	I didn't tell you everything.
Aaron	No?
Esther	It was too wild. It still seems unbelievable, even to me. Don't interrupt me, I beg you. I'm not completely healthy—I may even say that I'm sick—but I know the difference between fact and illusion. I haven't slept for nights. I keep wondering if I should call you or not. I decided not to—but this evening it occurred to me that if I couldn't trust you with a thing like this, then there's no one I can talk to. I read your books and I know you have a sense of the great mysteries ...

Esther says all this while stammering, with pauses. For a moment her eyes smile, then they turn sad, wavering.

Aaron	You can tell me everything.
Esther	I'm afraid you'll think me insane.
Aaron	I swear I will not.

Pause.

Esther	I want you to know that I saw Hitler.
Aaron	When? Where?
Esther	You see, you're frightened already. It happened three years ago. Here—on Broadway.
Aaron	On the street?
Esther	In the cafeteria.
Aaron	Esther, you must have seen someone resembling him. Hitler is dead.
Esther	I knew you would say that. But remember, you've promised to listen. You remember the fire in the cafeteria?
Aaron	Yes.
Esther	It has to do with the fire. Since you don't believe me anyway, why draw it out. It happened this way. That night I couldn't sleep. Usually, when I can't sleep, I get up and make tea, or try to read a book, but this time something made me get dressed and go out. I can't explain to you how I dared to walk on Broadway at that late hour. It must have been about two or three o'clock. I reached the cafeteria, thinking perhaps it stays open all night. I tried to look inside, but the window was covered by a large curtain. There was a pale light inside. So I tried revolving the door and it

turned. I saw a scene I will not forget to the end of my life. The tables were shoved together and around them sat men in white robes, like doctors or orderlies, all with swastikas on their sleeves. At the head sat Hitler. *Aaron looks shocked.* I beg you to hear me out—even a deranged person sometimes deserves to be listened to. At first they didn't see me. They were busy with the Führer. He started to talk. That terrible voice—I heard it many times on the radio. I didn't make out what he said. I was too terrified to take it in. Suddenly one of them looked at me and jumped up from his chair. How I came out alive I will never know. I ran with all my strength. When I got home, I said to myself, "Esther, you're not right in the head." The next morning I didn't go straight to work, but walked to the cafeteria to see if it was really there. Such an experience makes a person doubt his own senses. When I arrived I found the place had burned down. When I saw this, I knew it had to do with what I'd seen. Those who were there wanted all traces erased. These are the plain facts. I have no reason to fabricate such strange things.

Pause.

Aaron	*Hesitating.* Esther. You had a vision.
Esther	What do you mean, a vision?
Aaron	The past is not lost. An image from years ago remained present somewhere in the fourth dimension and it reached you just at that moment.
Esther	As far as I know, Hitler never wore a long white robe.
Aaron	Perhaps he did. I haven't seen every photograph ever taken.
Esther	Why did the cafeteria burn down just that night?
Aaron	Perhaps the fire evoked the vision.
Esther	There was no fire then. Somehow I foresaw you would give me this kind of explanation. If this was a vision, my sitting here with you is also a vision.
Aaron	How could it have been anything else? Even if Hitler is living and hiding out in the United States, he is not likely to meet his cronies at a cafeteria on Broadway. Besides, the cafeteria belongs to a Jew.
Esther	I saw him as I am seeing you now.
Aaron	You had a glimpse back into time.
Esther	Well, let it be so. But since then I have had no rest. I keep thinking about it. If I am destined to lose my mind, this will drive me to it.

Aaron	What about the psychiatrist your lawyer sent you to? Tell it to him and you'll get full compensation.
Esther	I know what you mean. I haven't fallen that low yet.

8. The cafeteria. Aaron and Lieberman at a table.

Liberman	If time and space are nothing more than forms of perception, so argues Kant, and quality, quantity, and causality are only categories of thinking, why shouldn't Hitler confer with his Nazis in a cafeteria on Broadway.
Aaron	How can the brain produce such nightmares? How do I know the same thing won't happen to me? Or you.
Lieberman	Perhaps it already has. I sometimes think I have already become one of those who are not seen by others. Sometimes I have the feeling that I'm already a corpse. *He smiles at Aaron.* You should pay more attention to your books, Aaron. You should be made to read them *after* publication, like the rest of us. And not just before.
Aaron	*Smiling back.* I've always wished I could. Anyway, at least once.
Lieberman	Perhaps I know more about your books than you do. You're telling us, always, humanity suffers from schizophrenia.

I begin to believe you. Perhaps you're right. Perhaps, along with the atom, the personality of *Homo sapiens* has also been splitting. When it comes to technology, the brain still functions, but in everything else degeneration has already begun.

Avrom, the ex-Stalinist, passes the table with his bowl of rice pudding and cup of coffee. The pockets of his overcoat are stuffed with papers. He looks sullenly at Lieberman who returns his gaze. Briefly.

Lieberman   They're all insane: the Communists, the Fascists, the preachers of democracy, the writers, painters, clergy, atheists. Soon technology, too, will disintegrate. Buildings will collapse. Power plants will stop creating electricity. Generals will drop atomic bombs on their own populations. Insane revolutionaries will riot. I often think it will begin in New York. This metropolis has all the symptoms of a mind gone berserk.

9. The subway. Aaron descends the steps. A few people pass him in the passage. Suddenly Esther turns into the passage from an entrance. She is with a man. They are arm in arm. She looks radiant. She is wearing a new coat and hat. The man walks away without looking at Aaron. Esther smiles and nods to Aaron, who is very surprised.

Aaron turns as if to go after them. But when he turns, they have gone and there is no one else in the passageway. They could have turned into a near exit. Or have simply vanished into thin air. Aaron pauses for a moment and then hurries on in the direction he had been going, with a slight feeling of unreality.

10. On the train. Aaron sits in the corner of the carriage. He looks drawn and tired. He rests his head against the wall of the carriage and closes his eyes.

11. The cafeteria. Aaron is at the counter. Lieberman and another man are seated at a table. Aaron crosses and joins them.

Lieberman	Aaron.
Aaron	David. *To the other man.* Rabbi.

Aaron sits.

Rabbi	No longer.
Aaron	What do you mean?
Rabbi	You don't know?
Aaron	Know what?
Lieberman	He became agnostic.
Aaron	For such a man that must have been difficult.
Rabbi	Suddenly it became easy. So. I'm out of work. If you can think of any suitable occupation for an ex-Rabbi, be sure to tell me.

Aaron	*Smiles sympathetically. Stirs his coffee. After a slight pause.* You remember a girl called Esther?
Rabbi	Esther?
Aaron	*To Lieberman.* David, you must remember her.

Lieberman shrugs.

Aaron	You must. How often do we get young people here? This is a place for the elderly.
Rabbi	The pretty little woman who used to come here?
Aaron	Yes.
Rabbi	I heard she committed suicide.
Aaron	When—how?
Rabbi	I don't know. Some time ago.
Aaron	But I just saw her. Recently.
Rabbi	Perhaps we aren't talking about the same person after all.
Aaron	When she first came here, she was full of life. All the old men loved her.
Lieberman	I remember.
Aaron	*To the Rabbi.* This girl, the girl you're thinking of. How did she do it?
Rabbi	All I know is what I've heard. Some young woman who used to come here turned on the gas and made an end of herself. But whether we are talking

	about the same person, I can't be sure.
Aaron	Only recently I saw her arm in arm with someone I used to know twenty years ago. But I've forgotten his name. *To Lieberman.* You remember that café on East Broadway?

Lieberman nods.

Aaron	Where we used to gather? He'd sit at the table and give long lectures. In Europe, he had a reputation as a politician.
Lieberman	I remember who you mean. He chain smoked and dropped ash on the plates from which we ate.
Aaron	What was his name?
Lieberman	That I can't remember. But I remember he was angry with the new writers, and belittled the old ones.
Aaron	How old is he now? He must have been in his late eighties then, or even in his nineties. But when I saw him with Esther, he didn't look so old.
Lieberman	I thought I read somewhere that he was dead.
Aaron	Are you sure?
Lieberman	It's a long time since I've been sure of anything.

Aaron	Then if he's dead, it means that Esther, too, is not alive.
Rabbi	I only know what I've heard.

12. The train. Aaron opens his eyes, gazes out of the window.

Narration: "I decided not to rest until I knew for certain what had happened to Esther and that half writer, half politician. But I grew busier from day to day. The cafeteria closed. The neighborhood changed. Years passed and I never saw or heard of Esther again. Yes, corpses do walk on Broadway. But why did Esther choose that particular corpse? She could have gotten a better bargain even in this world."

Aaron remains very still as he gazes out the window.

www.ingramcontent.com/pod-product-compliance
Lightning Source LLC
LaVergne TN
LVHW051611080426
835510LV00020B/3246